Who is this book...?

This booklet is for students taking GCSEs.

How can it help?

The aims of this booklet are:

✓ to boost your confidence
✓ to give you lots of ideas about how to revise
✓ to help you to make the most of your time

What's in it?

WARNING!
DO NOT READ THIS BOOKLET
FROM START TO FINISH.
Dip into it when you need to!

Using this booklet

Do

✓ Flick through the booklet to see what each of the sections is about.

✓ Try out any new ideas that appeal to you and don't be afraid to change the new ideas to suit you.

✓ Add any new ideas to the ways you already have for revising.

✓ Try out the new ideas when you get bogged down with your revision.

✓ Keep this booklet in a handy place throughout your revision and dip into it from time to time to give your revision a boost.

✓ Have a pen or highlighter handy as you are reading and highlight the ideas you like as you go along.

✓ Start by thinking about the areas of revision you would like some help with.

Don't

✗ Stop using any of your own methods if they have worked for you in the past.

✗ Read the booklet through from start to finish.

1
Doing your
REVISION

> *The best revision methods involve being active.
> So don't just sit there – DO SOMETHING!*

Active or passive revision?

- Active revision means involving your eyes, ears and hands in a variety of ways. Revising actively is the best way to make sense of the material you're revising and also helps you to remember it.

- Active methods of revision include: writing revision notes, reading notes aloud, recording key points onto your phone, discussing topics with a friend, testing yourself, getting others to test you, rewriting notes, doing examples, trying past exam papers and using revision websites. Use as many of these methods as you find useful.

- Passively reading through your notes and books is a very poor method of revision. It doesn't help you to understand or remember what you are revising. Don't just sit there reading page after page until you get bored!

Revise with the exam in mind

- Get hold of the exam board specification (syllabus) for each subject. Ask your teacher for the specification or download it from the exam board website. You can use this as a basis for which topics to revise.

- For each subject make sure you know how many papers you have to take, how many questions you have to answer, what choice of questions you have (if any), what type of questions are asked, how long the exam is and when it is.

- Revision isn't just about learning facts and information. It's also vital that you are able to use this knowledge to answer exam questions. Tackling past papers is a great way to improve your exam technique.

- When working through past papers you can write complete answers or outline answers using your revision cards or notes. Writing an outline answer means putting down just the main ideas and points without writing full sentences or all the details. Doing outline answers is a good way to practice essay-type questions.

- Some of your revision time should be devoted to practising under exam conditions. This means putting away your books and turning off your music. Try out sample questions as if you were in the exam and see how well you do. Get used to working at high speed for long periods of time because that's what you'll be doing in most exams. The more timed questions you do, the better you'll get at doing them.

- Try having at least one session which goes nonstop for the full time that the exam will take in the weeks leading up to the exam. As the exam gets closer try out more sample questions under exam conditions.

- You will face different types of exam questions for each subject. You should try to adjust your revision to the subject and the types of questions you will meet in each particular exam. Keep your mind focused on possible exam questions.

Writing your own revision notes

- Writing revision notes is a great way of being active in your revision. It is also a positive method for tackling bulging folders and exercise books full of notes.

- Revision notes should be created in the early stages of your revision. Don't attempt to memorise all your lesson notes – condense them first.

- Revision notes are useful for any subject where you have to recall material. In writing revision notes you are picking out the most important points and trying to reduce the amount of information to a more manageable amount.

- Ways of making revision notes include: traditional revision notes on A4 file paper, revision cards and patterned notes. Select which method works best for you, often a combination of methods works best.

- Subject revision guides that you can buy in the shops are very helpful in your revision but you should not see them as a substitute for writing your revision notes. It is very important that you write your own revision notes.

Writing traditional revision notes

- Choose a topic or part of a topic that you want to revise. Look at "bite-size" chunks of work and don't try working with too large a topic at a time.

- Read through the notes you have on that topic, this may include looking at your folders, notebooks, text books and revision guides. As you are reading ask yourself, 'Do I understand this?'

- When you feel you have understood the topic, go back and pick out key words and phrases that trigger off your memory. Also pick out any important diagrams, tables, graphs and formulae. It's best to do this in rough to start with.

- Read through the rough notes you have just written, check they contain the important ideas and vital details and then write them out neatly.

- Pay attention to these points:

  ➢ Use your **own words.**

  ➢ Make sure your notes are well **spaced out** and don't cram too much onto a page.

  ➢ Use large writing and even better use **CAPITAL LETTERS**.

  ➢ Make your revision notes **interesting** by using colour, boxes, circles, underlining, abbreviations and so on.

Making revision cards

- Revision cards (or flashcards as some people call them) can be bought from supermarkets, stationery stores or online in a variety of sizes and colours and are known as record cards.

- Because of their small size they have some advantages over traditional notes. They can be carried around in a pocket or bag and can be used wherever you are and whenever you've got a spare moment. They contain only a small amount of information so you don't feel swamped when you look at them. As they contain only a small amount of information they don't take much time to rewrite if you need to.

- Pay careful attention to the following points:

  - Always draw a margin down the left hand side of each card, about 3cm from the edge. This is useful for adding extra notes when you need to.

  - Always write the subject in the top right hand corner of the card.

  - Always put a title at the top of the card.

  - Develop your own method for numbering the cards.

  - Don't be afraid to scrap a card and rewrite it if you are unhappy with it.

  - Cards covering the same subject or topic should be kept together. A good way of doing this is to use a piece of string or an elastic band tied through a hole in the left hand corner of the cards. Make the hole with a hole punch.

Creating patterned notes

- Some students find patterned notes more fun to do and more interesting to revise from. They are particularly good at giving you an overall view of a topic and for showing links and connections.

- Some other names you might come across for patterned notes are: mind map, spider diagram, brainstorm, learning map or concept map.

- To write patterned notes follow these steps:

  1) Write the **MAIN TOPIC** in the middle of the paper and draw a ring around it.

  2) For each **KEY POINT** draw a branch out from the main topic.

  3) Write a **KEY WORD** or **PHRASE** on each branch.

  4) Build out further branches and add **DETAILS**.
     - add diagrams, pictures and symbols where you can.
     - highlight links and connections.
     - be creative and personalise it.

Using your revision notes

During a revision session

- Choose a topic to revise and find your revision notes for this topic.

- Read the notes through, and as you do this try to recreate the whole topic in your mind.

- Place the notes face down and write out, or in the case of patterned notes redraw, what you can remember.

- Compare what you have written down to what is written in your notes and check for anything you may have missed out.

- If you have left out some important details, test yourself again.

- If you need extra detail you can always refer back to your original notes.

During spare moments

- Carry some of your revision cards around with you.

- You can read them on the bus, in the car, during lunchtime or break, when you are waiting in the corridor at school or during odd spare moments at home.

- After reading a revision card, try to recall the information in your mind.

- Ask friends, parents, brothers, sisters and anyone else who is willing, to test you using your revision cards.

How can I improve my memory?

- To most students (you, perhaps?) memorising normally involves reading and re-reading information in the hope that it will stick, even if you don't understand it. Unfortunately, this kind of repetition doesn't work very well and is boring. The 5 ideas below should help.

  1) Try to understand the information first. You will not be able to remember information if you do not understand why it's important or how it relates to the subject you are studying. Work hard to make sense of it and to see where it fits in.

2) Play around and create memory hooks which help you to remember things. Hooks work best when they're crazy, unusual, funny and YOURS! Use links, pictures, rhymes and stories to create hooks.

3) Get your senses involved. Use your eyes, ears and hands when you're trying to remember information – be active.

4) Recall the information regularly by testing yourself and getting others to test you. Remember, *use it or lose it.*

5) Take bite-size chunks of information and don't overload yourself. Work with small amounts at a time.

- Memory hooks come in handy when you have a list of things or a specific item to memorise. But use them sparingly as whilst they help you to remember, they don't help you to understand.

- One type of memory hook, called a mnemonic, uses the first letters from words you are trying to remember. For example, HOMES is a mnemonic which is used to remember the names of the five Great Lakes in Canada: **H**uron, **O**ntario, **M**ichigan, **E**erie, **S**uperior.

- Another type of memory hook is to take the first letter of a list of words and make a silly sentence with them. For instance, the directions of the compass North, East, South, West are recalled by using **N**aughty **E**lephants **S**quirt **W**ater.

- Pictures can be good memory hooks. When trying to remember a word in a foreign language draw a basic picture based on the word you want to remember and write the word next to the picture. You can also use this method to remember historical dates by drawing a picture which reminds you of what happened on that date and writing the date underneath. Stick these pictures up in your bedroom.

- Making a rhyme or song can make a good hook to remember a list of things. You can put it to the tune of a well known song or nursery rhyme, or even make up your own tune.

Even more ideas!

Let's get together

- Take full advantage of revision lessons at school. Your teachers are the best aid to revision you've got, listen to their advice and ask them lots of questions.

- Try organising a quiz with a friend. Before you get together write down 5 questions about a topic to ask each other.

- Ask family and friends to test you from your revision notes or try to explain a topic to them.

- Some students find it useful to arrange revision sessions with one or two friends who are doing the same exams. Before you get together, decide the subject and topic you're going to look at and decide how you're going to revise it. As well as looking at individual topics, you can swap and discuss answers to trial exam papers.

Terrific technology

- There are some great revision websites. Ask your teachers which ones they recommend or simply type the word 'revision' and the subject into your favourite search engine and see what comes up.

- There are also some fantastic revision videos which cover all sorts of things including lessons on specific topics, working through past papers, worked examples, revision methods, revision planning and exam technique. Ask your friends and teachers to recommend the best ones.

- Some websites allow you to download audio revision topics to your phone or iPOD.

- Using your phone or iPOD works very well for some students. Try reading out your revision notes and recording yourself, then play it back whenever you get the chance.

Testing, testing

- For important formulae, definitions, quotations, theories and ideas test yourself regularly.

- For formulae, definitions and quotations which you have to memorise, try reading and testing yourself just before you go to sleep and repeating this as soon as you wake up. Try also testing and rehearsing them more than you think necessary until you remember them 'parrot fashion'.

- When faced with having to learn a long list of items, such as foreign language vocabulary, try this:

  1) Learn the first two words on the list until you can write them out from memory.

  2) Add a third word and learn them all until you can write all three from memory.

  3) Add a fourth word and learn them all until you can write all four from memory and so on....

- When you are working on a list of items try using your fingers as a counter as you commit each one to memory.

Try these for size

- Write key points on sticky notes and stick them to things like a mirror, wardrobe, toilet door, stair banisters, kitchen cupboards and so on.

- Write giant-size notes on large sheets of paper and stick them up in your bedroom.

- Here's an unusual and effective idea. Select a few key topics from each subject and write them in large letters on some old strips of wallpaper. Hang them in your bedroom (on your ceiling, perhaps!) so that you look at them often but make sure you change the topics from time to time.

- In subjects where people are involved, such as English Literature and History, imagine what it would be like to meet the characters. Ask yourself how you would react to the situations they faced in their life, what would it be like to live in their community and what you would think of the people around them.

- When working through past exams why not try starting with the last question and working backwards through the paper!

2

Drawing up your
REVISION TIMETABLE

*There's quite a lot of revision time available
— if you manage it well!*

About revision timetables

Getting underway

- There are many good reasons for using revision timetables.
  These include:
  - ✓ To avoid a last minute rush the night before an exam.
  - ✓ To set up a routine and discipline yourself.
  - ✓ To share revision time between subjects.
  - ✓ To keep up with your revision.
  - ✓ To spread out your revision.
  - ✓ To get the right balance between revision and leisure time.
  - ✓ To avoid wasting time trying to decide what to do for each revision session.

- Before you start your revision draw up a chart showing the dates and times of all your exams and work out how many weeks until your first exam.

- The first step in planning your revision is to decide when you are going to start. This will depend on whether you are preparing for Pre-Public Exams, mock (trial) exams or the final exams.

- There is no 'correct' time to start your revision, this is something for you to decide. As a guideline, for your final exams in the summer you should start serious revision about 6-8 weeks before your first exam – even if this means spending just a few hours in the early weeks. If for any reason you start later, don't panic as the guidance given here is still valid.

What goes wrong with timetables?

- There are 3 main reasons why timetables don't work out:

  ➢ They are drawn up to cover too many weeks ahead.

  ➢ They are drawn up in too much detail.

  ➢ They are over-ambitious and unrealistic.

- Timetables can work for everyone and a good timetable is one that strikes the right balance between flexibility and routine.

- Revision timetables are not meant to tie you down in a rigid way but can be an excellent tool to help guide you through your revision period.

- If you are like most students, you will never stick exactly to your timetables and when you don't it doesn't mean that your timetables aren't working. Allow yourself some flexibility and don't worry if you don't do everything you planned to do.

Drawing up a timetable

- There are many ways to divide up the day. One simple way is to divide each day into three blocks: morning, afternoon and evening. There are no exact times for when a block of time starts but a rough guide is:

  morning session   9.00am – 1.00pm
  afternoon session   1.00pm – 5.00pm
  evening session   5.00pm – 9.00pm

- Another way is to divide up the day into 1 hour blocks. For example 9-10am, 10-11am right through until 8-9pm.

- These are only suggestions and you will need to divide up the day in a way that suits you as you may want to start earlier or finish later or maybe organise your day into 2 hour blocks.

What steps do I follow in drawing up a timetable?

Step 1)   Draw up a trial timetable lasting one week.
Step 2)   Work through your trial timetable.
Step 3)   Review your trial timetable.
Step 4)   Draw up a timetable for the next week and work through it.
Step 5)   Review the timetable.
Step 6)   Draw up your next timetable.

Now repeat steps 5 and 6 until you have sat your last exam.

In the centre pages of this booklet are 2 different timetables. Pick the one you like best, pull it out, copy it and don't forget to use it!

For tips and ideas on how to draw up a revision timetable turn to page 17.

THU	FRI	SAT	SUN

Weekly Revision Timetable

	MON	TUE	WED
8:00am			
9:00am			
10:00am			
11:00am			
12:00am			
1:00pm			
2:00pm			
3:00pm			
4:00pm			
5:00pm			
6:00pm			
7:00pm			
8:00pm			

THU	FRI	SAT	SUN

Weekly Revision Timetable

	MON	TUE	WED
Morning			
Afternoon			
Evening			

Drawing up a trial timetable

- Make a list of the subjects for which you are taking exams.

- Get enough copies of blank revision timetables to cover your revision and the exam period (see centre pages for timetable pull-outs).

- The first timetable you draw up should only cover the first week from the date you start your revision. This is a trial period to enable you to find out how much revision you can realistically do. For this one week trial period enter the dates on your timetable.

- Enter all your commitments such as lessons, time you will need to complete any unfinished coursework, controlled assessments or other study, clubs and most importantly, time to relax! For weeks in which you have exams, these should also be entered on your timetable.

- When drawing up a revision timetable consider the following ideas:
  - ➢ leave time for leisure activities
  - ➢ balance revision time between your subjects
  - ➢ space out the revision for each subject over the week
  - ➢ vary the subjects revised on each day.

- Pin up your timetable in a prominent place in your room.

Drawing up your next timetable

- When you come to the end of each weekly timetable, carry out a quick review and draw up a timetable for the next week.

- Repeat this cycle of drawing up a timetable and reviewing it until you have sat your last exam.

- Always stick up your timetables where you can see them!

3

Organising your
REVISION SESSIONS

*You'll learn most if you use your
revision time effectively!*

Where do I start?

Making a topic checklist

- For each subject, make a list of the major topics you have covered - this list is called a topic checklist. A topic checklist is a kind of route map showing you a path through your revision. If you find it difficult to list the topics you have studied ask your subject teachers for help. If you have the exam board specification (this includes a list of the topics that might come up in the exam) this can be helpful in checking what you have covered.

- For each subject, look at the topics and decide what order you want to tackle them in. Pick a topic you like or find easy to start with as this boosts your confidence. You don't have to revise the topics in the same order you were taught them.

- Pin up your topic checklists in your bedroom or keep them in an easily accessible place.

Using your topic checklist

- When you start a revision session look at your revision timetable to find out which subject you have chosen to revise. Then look at your topic checklist to find out which topic you have chosen to tackle next.

- After each revision session, tick off the topic from your checklist (but only if you are happy that you have covered it adequately). This will help you to see the progress you are making and help you feel more in control. It will also stop you from feeling that you're not getting anywhere.

Organising your time

Getting the basics right

- Spend 5-10 minutes at the beginning of each day making a plan for the day ahead. This may involve checking your revision timetable or if you're not using one thinking about the subjects to revise.

- Set a definite time to start and finish each session and stick to it.

- Put your phone in a different room. Put your phone in a different room. This is not a typo, this has been repeated as it's vital that you don't allow yourself to be tempted by the distractions your phone offers! If your phone is nearby you will look at it so PUT IT IN A DIFFERENT ROOM!!

- If you are using a tablet or laptop to help with revision you will have to exercise some self-discipline. Resist the temptation to respond to every message, notification or alert you might get. Don't leave social media tabs or apps open. When watching videos use full screen to avoid clicking on other links.

- Keep revision sessions to a reasonable length. Between 1-3 hours is about right.

- Try to work in good light. You might get a headache if the light you work in is poor.

- Most people are at their best in the morning. Try working on difficult topics in the morning when your mind is fresh.

- If you are going to listen to music, play it at low volume and choose something that doesn't distract you. If you find yourself singing along, then you are distracted! When you have a break, try playing loud and lively music.

Improving your concentration

- If you find it difficult to concentrate for long periods of time, start with short sessions and gradually build up to longer sessions.

- Make sure you have regular breaks. How often and how long these breaks are will depend on how long you are revising for, the material you are revising, the time of day and your own concentration span. A good guide is that for every hour you work, have a break of 10 minutes. You may find that a break after every 20 or 30 minutes works best for you.

- You do not necessarily have to get up from your chair every time you have a break, often it is better to just sit and daydream for a few minutes. Experiment with your breaks, be flexible and find out what works best for you.

- You may find it helps with your concentration if you vary the topic or the subject during each session.

- If your school offers revision classes take full advantage of them. This is particularly helpful when it's difficult to get peace and quiet at home.

- Walking around whilst reading or testing yourself can help concentration.

- Just getting up and moving around or simply changing your sitting position can sometimes help concentration.

Even more ideas!

- Always end a revision session by summing up or testing yourself. An effective revision session might be divided up like this: 40 minutes revising, 10 minutes testing, 10 minutes resting. If you have a short attention span try 20 minutes revising, 5 minutes testing, 5 minutes resting. Short bursts like this can be useful when you're tired or the topic is difficult.

- Keep a bottle of water nearby when you are revising and take regular sips. Small levels of dehydration can reduce your mental performance.

- Clear your desk or table of everything except for relevant material and equipment and put away anything that might distract you.

- To help you get the right balance between your subjects you may find it useful to keep track of the time you spend revising. You could do this by making a note on your revision timetable of how many hours you revise in each session or keep a revision diary.

- Give yourself something to look forward to or some kind of reward after revision sessions - go on, spoil yourself!

- One final thought here. When the exams start you may be tempted to think that revision is finished. However, the periods between exams give you vital additional time to top-up your revision. Naturally, you will need to relax after each exam but if you have other exams coming up get back to revising as soon as you can.

4

Going for the
TOP GRADES

Getting the top grades is all about hard work
- a lot of effort over a long period of time.

Make revision a priority

- In the period leading up to the final exams make revision your top priority. Stay focused on the task of giving yourself the best possible preparation for the exams that lie ahead. Other things can wait until the exams are finished.

Start early

- Start revising months rather than weeks before your first exam. Begin with a small amount of revision each week and gradually build up the number of hours.

Put in the hours

- There is no escaping the fact that in order to get the top grades you will have to put in long (and often boring) hours of work. This is particularly true if you want to get high grades in a lot of different subjects.

Revise all topics

- To give yourself the best chance of achieving the top grades try not to have any 'no-go' areas. In most of your subjects there will have been topics you found difficult when they were covered in class. Target these topics early in your revision and work hard to understand them. Use the specification for each subject to check which topics to cover.

Tackle past papers

- It goes without saying that working through lots of past papers is important but there's much more to gain from doing this than simply getting used to exam questions. Use past papers as a way of finding out gaps in your understanding. Once you've identified these gaps revise these topics thoroughly. This is a repeating cycle of tackling a past paper, checking your answers, identifying gaps in your understanding, revising those topics then tackling another past paper and so on.

Take every opportunity to revise

- Revision is a skill that needs practising, the more you do it the better you get. Make it a habit right from the beginning of your GCSE courses to take every opportunity to revise. Revise for classroom tests, end of unit tests, end of year exams and especially pre-public exams and mocks. If your school runs revision sessions at lunchtime, after-school, on Saturdays or during holidays go to them.

Use the exam board websites

- Make visits to the exam board websites a regular part of your revision. On them you will find the specification for each subject (a list of the topics you need to cover and details of the exams), past papers, mark schemes and information on grade boundaries. Check with your teacher which exam board each subject is taken with and the exact specification you are working to.

5

Sitting your
EXAMS

*Exams measure not only what you know,
but how well you take them!*

The night before

- Only attempt light revision using your revision notes and try not to do any totally new revision.

- Get all the equipment you will need (pens, rulers, calculators etc) ready the night before. The last thing you want in the morning is to be rushing around trying to find things.

- Try to get a normal night's sleep (if you can!).

On the day

- Get up in plenty of time.

- When you leave home make sure you've got with you everything you need for the exam.

- If you want to, do some last minute revision by flicking through your revision notes.

- Don't spend too long waiting outside the exam room as this can make you feel more nervous than you already are. Make an agreement with your friends not to talk about the exam.

Compose yourself

- The moment you first open your exam paper is always a bit of a shock. The exam never looks or reads quite the way you expect it to, so be prepared for this.

- Don't worry about your classmates who may already be scribbling away.

- If necessary, begin by taking a couple of minutes to write down anything you are afraid of forgetting.

- If you are the sort of person who freezes in exams or finds that your mind goes blank, it may be better for you to get writing as quickly as possible so that you can get your ideas flowing.

Read the instructions carefully

- Read the whole paper through carefully, noting all the instructions given about the number and choice of questions.

- If you have a choice of questions, select and mark those questions you feel confident that you are able to answer well.

- Decide on your question order then start by answering the questions you know you can answer well. This gives you more time to think about the difficult questions and boosts your confidence.

- It can be a mistake to tackle difficult questions first, as you might run out of time to do the questions you can answer more easily and fully.

- One of the most common ways that pupils fail is simply by not answering the right number of questions.

Budget your time

- Always take a watch in with you.

- Before the day of the exam, work out roughly how much time you can devote to each question or section. This will depend on: how much time you have for the whole exam, the total number of questions, the type and difficulty of each question and the marks given to each question.

- You may wish to write down approximate finishing times for each question or section to help you see the progress you are making, so take a watch in with you.

- As you're taking the exam, you may find yourself falling behind the schedule you set for yourself. Don't panic, simply work a little faster.

- Don't fall into the trap of spending the most time trying to answer the questions about which you know very little.

Tackle the questions

- Read every question at least twice, picking out key words. If it helps, underline the key words.

- Think about the question and analyse it before you get into your answer. Get a sense of how long and detailed an answer is expected.

- For essay-type questions outline the main points you intend to include in your answer. Without an outline you are likely to stray from the point or forget important points.

- Remember to stick to what the question is asking!

6

Coping with your
STRESS

*Everybody gets nervous, but you can
learn to reduce your nerves.*

Talk about it

- Think about the people you know who will listen to you and make sure you talk to them. Your listeners can be friends, family, teachers or others.

- Asking for help is not a sign of weakness. It is a sign of maturity and strength to realise when you have difficulties and to feel confident enough to share those difficulties with others.

Take time out to have fun

- During the revision period make sure you give yourself some time to do the things you enjoy. Do the things that relax you and take your mind off your studies.

Do some exercise

- One of the best ways of dealing with stress is to exercise as you will find that after exercising your muscles are relaxed and calm.

- Exercise also helps to clear the mind.

- Exercise provides a way of releasing a great deal of the muscle tension which stress produces.

Think positively

- A lot of exam success can be put down to positive thinking. Thinking you might fail drains away your confidence, makes you worry more and makes you less enthusiastic about working hard.

- Don't tell yourself things like, 'I'm useless at this subject' or 'I haven't got enough time to revise properly'. Replace this unhelpful self-talk with statements like, 'This subject is difficult but I've had difficult subjects before and understood them' or 'I can get my revision done in time when I plan a proper revision timetable'.

Relax your muscles

- Muscle relaxation doesn't simply mean doing nothing with your muscles; it involves tensing and relaxing them.

- Start by tensing and then relaxing the muscles around the head, face, neck and shoulders. Then work down your body tensing and relaxing your arms, hands, chest, back, stomach, hips, legs and feet.

Eat well

- Eating well reduces the overall stress on the body and can also make you feel good about yourself. Try eating a variety of foods.

Use breathing techniques

- Here is step-by-step approach to help you relax:

  1) Sit comfortably and close your eyes.
  2) Breathe in slowly though your nose to the count of ten.
  3) Hold this breath while you count to ten again.
  4) Now let out your breath slowly and count to ten once more.
  5) Repeat this three times.

  You can use this technique at any time when you feel nervous, such as on exam days.

Use mental imagery

- Mental imagery is a bit like a daydream and can help you relax your mind.

- Start by getting yourself comfortable. Close your eyes and start to breathe deeply, concentrating all the time on your breathing.

- Now form a picture in your mind of a pleasant scene such as a tropical island, a valley, a woodland area. Try to include smells and sounds.

- Explore the scene and enjoy the surroundings. When you are ready, slowly open your eyes.

7

How PARENTS can help

> *Don't compare your own experiences of exams and revision with that of your children's!*

It goes without saying that all children are different, so it follows that there is no single approach to how a parent can help out, but here are some suggestions.

Do

✓ Discuss with your child what will be involved in the revision period and what your role could be.

✓ Provide the environment necessary for success. Ideally, they need a quiet, well-lit place to study with interruptions kept to a minimum when they are working.

✓ Respond positively when they ask for help. Ask exactly how you can help and if you can't help immediately say when it's convenient.

✓ Give plenty of praise and encouragement, stay calm and don't expect too much.

✓ Keep them well supplied with food and drinks.

✓ Keep a low profile.

✓ Be prepared to listen when they want to talk about problems as everything becomes more emotional and heightened during the exam period.

✓ Encourage them to take regular breaks during long periods of revision.

✓ Encourage morning revision when the brain is more receptive and discourage studying right up to bedtime.

Don't

✗ Make comparisons with brothers, sisters, their friends and so on.

✗ Unintentionally add to their worries by constantly mentioning the exams.

✗ Relate too much to when you were sitting exams at school or how you did your revision.

✗ Worry if their revision techniques seem strange or unusual.

✗ Make a battleground out of whether or not they listen to music when doing their revision.

✗ Distract them unnecessarily.

✗ Expect them to study all the time as taking some time out to relax will have a positive effect on their work.

And finally..........

TRY OUT some of the tips.

ENJOY your revision.

It's up to **YOU** now.

I wish you every **SUCCESS!**

GO FOR IT!!!